Britta Teckentrup

THE EGG

PRESTEL   Munich · London · New York

The Egg

A Miracle of Nature

The egg has always played a major part
in our culture. Since the beginning of
time the egg has been an object of
fascination to humankind. It has been
worshipped in religion and mythology
as the source of all life around the world.
Because of its perfect shape, sensual
feel and beautiful colours, it is treasured
as one of the most perfect objects in
the universe.

Curvaceous Perfection

An egg is fragile and strong at the same time—ordinary and extraordinary.

To the human brain the perfect continuity of curvature is the most pleasing shape there is. Even though an egg might look fragile, it has a very strong structure.

If you squeeze an egg lengthwise it is quite hard to crack. The reason for this toughness is the curvaceous shape of the egg.

You can compare it to the strong structure of an arch in architecture.

Eggs have to support the weight of the adult bird, and a chicken egg can support an object as heavy as a large book.

Egg Collections

Bird eggs have always been highly desirable objects and were widely collected, especially around the time of English naturalist Charles Darwin, who studied birds in the 1800s.

Eggs were collected for scientific purposes, often to learn more about the diversity of nature.

Eggs were even sold and displayed as beautiful, valuable curiosities.

In 1954, after people learned that egg collecting was threatening bird populations, the United Kingdom outlawed its practice.

Today some specimens are still collected for scientific research, and you can see many fascinating egg collections in museums worldwide.

Bird Eggs

Oology

When we talk about the beauty of eggs we
mainly talk about the large variety of bird eggs.
The study of bird eggs is called Oology, which
is a branch of Ornithology—the study of birds.
Oology deals mainly with the description,
appearance and categorising of eggs, which
includes form, weight, texture and colour.

Egg Shapes

Bird eggs vary greatly in size and shape.
Most bird eggs have an oval shape, with one
end rounded and the other more pointed.
The shape of the egg is related to the habitat
of the bird.
Cliff-nesting birds often have highly
conical eggs. They are less likely to roll off
the nest, tending instead to roll around
in a tight circle. Many ground-nesting birds
have nearly round eggs.

Egg Colour

One of the most beautiful and striking features of
bird eggs is their colouration.

For even though many eggs are white, eggs of
virtually every colour are known.

The colour of an egg is mainly determined by genetics.

Eggshells can be intricately marked with speckles,
blotches or streaks.

These markings tend to become more dense around
the large end of the egg.

Pigment glands inside the bird add the colour and
markings to the egg.

Camouflage, age, habitat and even stress also play a
part in the colouration of eggs. In some cases the colour
helps the parents identify their eggs, especially where
large colonies of birds nest together.

The shell colour of a freshly laid egg can still be rubbed
off and only becomes permanent once the pigment
has set.

Different Coloured Eggs

The Blue Tit

Light cream with light brown speckles

Egg size: 1.6 x 1.2 cm

(0.63 x 0.47 in.)

House Sparrow

White to light grey eggs with grey-brown markings.

Egg size: 2.2 x 1.6 cm

(0.86 x 0.63 in.)

The Chaffinch

Off-white eggs with brown-red splotches

Egg size: 1.9 x 1.5 cm (0.75 x 0.59 in.)

Song Thrush

Light blue eggs with black markings.

Egg size: 2.7 x 2 cm (1.06 x 0.79 in.)

The Blackbird

Blue-green eggs with brown speckles

Egg size: 2.9 x 2.1 cm (1.14 x 0.83 in.)

The Robin

American robin chicks often hatch from vividly turquoise-coloured eggs.

An American robin (right page) is very different from its European cousin (below).

In fact the two birds are not related at all.

The American robin belongs to the thrush family.

When English settlers encountered the American robin with its red chest,

the bird reminded them of the robin they knew from back home and

they gave it the same name.

In contrast to the turquoise eggs of an American robin, the European robin's

eggs are cream or white and speckled or blotched with reddish-brown colour.

Camouflage

The colour and markings of an egg also help to camouflage it.

Most shorebirds, for example, lay their eggs in a scrape on a beach.

The speckles and blotches on the eggshell mimic the pebbles and textures of the beach perfectly and protect the egg from predators.

Inside the Egg

Anatomy

An egg is a perfect external incubation system.
The eggshell is a little wonder of nature – it is
thin and strong at the same time.
It has to be strong to withstand outside forces and
thin enough for the chick to be able to hatch.
If you look at an eggshell under a microscope, you'll
see that it's made up almost entirely of strong, compact
crystals.
Tiny pores in the eggshell let air pass through and
allow the embryo to breathe.
The shell also has a thin coating called the cuticle
that helps keep out bacteria and dust.
The egg yolk provides nutrients / food, and the egg white
protects the chick.
Tiny, twisted strips called chalazae hold the yolk
in the centre of the egg.

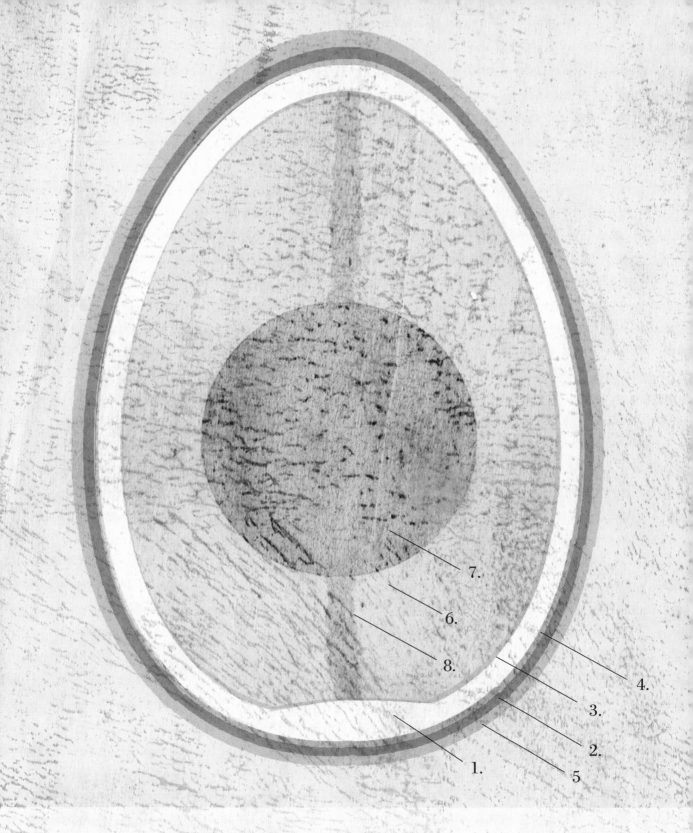

7.

6.

8.

4.

3.

2.

1.

5.

1. Air Space

2. Shell

3. Inner Shell Membrane

4. Outer Shell Membrane

5. Cuticle

6. Egg White

7. Yolk

8. Chalazae

Inside the Egg

Development of a Chick

A hen lays roughly 300 eggs per year.
If the egg is fertilised an embryo will develop.
The chicken egg starts inside the hen as
an egg yolk. It takes about a day for the egg
to be fully formed and laid.
The hen will sit on her eggs to keep them
warm so that they can hatch into chicks.
The chicken embryo develops inside the
egg for 21 days (a time called the incubation
period).
The chick will then peck its way out of its
eggshell and become hatched.

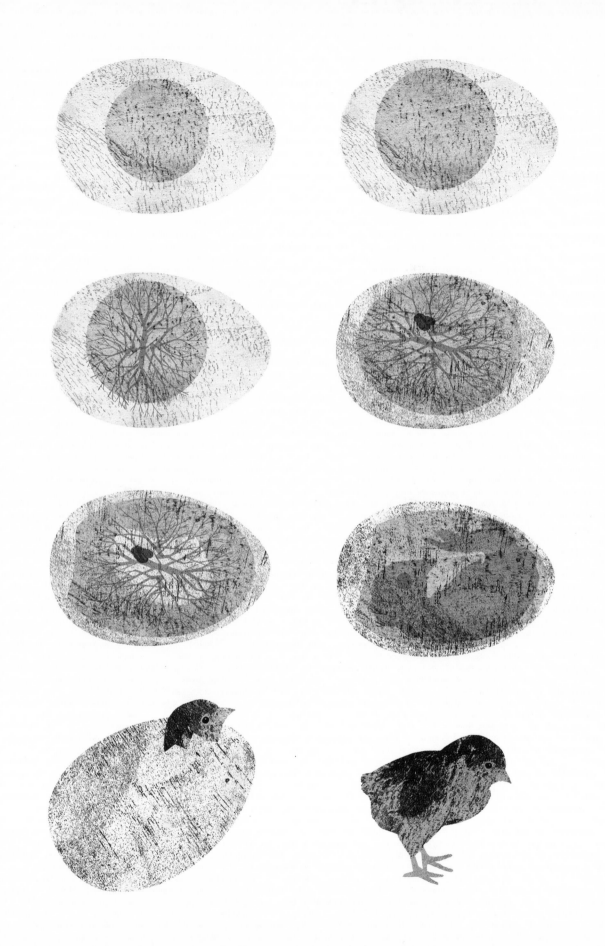

The Elephant Bird

The largest eggs ever laid were those of the
Elephant bird. Elephant birds were giant,
flightless birds that lived on the island of
Madagascar until about 1700. These creatures
were over three meters tall and were believed
to be the largest flightless birds ever to have
lived on Earth.

Surprisingly, recent research suggests
that the closest living relative of the Elephant
bird is the Kiwi, a smallish bird native to
New Zealand.

Real-Sized Elephant Bird Egg

An elephant bird egg is estimated to be about 34 cm (13.39 in.) long with a circumference of almost one meter (39.37 in.) and a weight of 10 kg (22.05 pounds). You could almost fit 160 hen eggs inside it.

The Hummingbird

The Smallest Egg

The smallest egg is that of a hummingbird,
only about 10 mm (0.39 in.) in length.
This egg is roughly the size of a coffee bean.

Hummingbirds are among the smallest of birds,
most species measuring 7.5-13 cm (2.95-5.12 in.).
They create a high-pitched humming sound by
beating their wings up to 50 times per second.
Hummingbirds can hover in the air whilst
drinking nectar from flowers with their long,
sometimes arched beaks.
Hummingbirds are spectacular-looking birds and
come in many beautiful colours and markings.

The Ostrich Egg

The African ostrich egg is the largest egg of a living
bird and one of the most treasured eggs of all.
It is almost round with a very thick eggshell and
a rough white surface.

1.   3.

Egg Sizes in Comparison

2.

4.

5.

1. Elephant Bird   3. Emu   5. Hummingbird

2. Ostrich   4. Chicken

Nests

Caliology (the study of bird's nests)

There are many different types of nests.
Some birds build their nests on the ground,
while others build them high up on trees,
mountains or rooftops.
There are floating nests, mounds nests,
cup nests, scrape nests, pendant nests and
sphere nests – each adapted perfectly to
the bird's environment. Some eggs are
hatched in a burrow or in the cavity of a
tree, on a ledge or on a platform. Some
birds build their nests on their own and
others in large colonies.
Some birds have no nests at all.

Masterful Nest Builders

The Baya Weaver Bird

Some birds are real masters at nest building.
One of these birds is the Baya weaver bird.
Baya weavers like to build their nest suspended
from a tree over open water to be safe from
predators.
The male weaves a delicate interwoven structure
out of grass strips, which the female inspects.
If she is happy with his nest building skills
she will mate with him.
Weaver birds like to build their nests in colonies.
The Baya weaver bird's eggs are white.

Pouch Nest

Oriole

The Baltimore Oriole's nest is built by
the female. It is a tightly woven hanging
pouch located on the end of a branch
hanging down on the underside. She
anchors her nest high in a tree.
Building the nest takes about a week.
The eggs are pale grey or blue-white
blotched with brown, black or lavender.

Mound Nest

Flamingo

Flamingos build nest mounds made of mud, small stones, straw and feathers. These mounds can be as high as 30 cm (11.81 in.) and have scooped-out tops for the egg.

The mound nests of flamingos help to protect their egg from fluctuating water levels.

Flamingos breed in large colonies with all chicks hatching at roughly the same time.

The male and female build their nest together and usually lay just one egg.

The egg of a flamingo is chalky white.

Cavity Nest

The Woodpecker

Woodpeckers nest in holes and cavities
that they excavate in trees.
Eggs of cavity-nesting birds, such as
woodpeckers, are often white.
These eggs are hidden from predators,
so they have no need for colouring that
camouflages them. The brightness of
the eggs may help the parents locate
them more easily in the cavity.

Mud Nest

The Cliff Swallow

Cliff swallows build clusters of mud nests
and breed in colonies.
Their nests are often attached to vertical walls.
Their natural habitats for nest building are
cliffs, but they also build many of their nests
in man-made structures.
The cliff swallow collects small chunks of
mud and uses them like bricks for its nest
building. One nest can contain over 1000 mud pellets.
The egg of a cliff swallow is off-white with
brownish speckles.

Ground Nest

Snowy Owl

The snowy owl builds a circular shallow
nest bowl on snow-free ground during the
Arctic summer.
The female lays from three to eleven eggs
and incubates them for about a month.
The male feeds the female while she sits
on the nest and keeps the eggs warm and safe.
Snowy owl eggs are a glossy white.

Burrow Nesting Birds

Kingfisher

A hole in the ground or a river bank may seem a strange place to find a bird nest, but underground burrows are home to quite a few bird species. Kingfishers build nesting burrows on the banks of rivers and streams. The nest tunnel is usually 60-90 cm (23.62-35.43 in.) long. Kingfisher eggs are a glossy white. Kiwis also lay their egg in a burrow. They lay just one large single egg, which is the largest egg in proportion to body size in the bird kingdom.

Cliff Nesting

Guillemots

Unlike birds that incubate their young in carefully
built nests, sea-loving guillemots lay their eggs in rather
dangerous and exposed places like rock ledges and cliffs.
They breed in large and very crowded colonies on
islands and coastlines throughout the North Atlantic
and North Pacific Oceans. The conical shape of
guillemot eggs prevents them from falling off the cliffs.
This highly adapted shape makes the egg spin in a tight
circle in case it gets knocked over.
Guillemots' eggs have a waterproof and self-cleaning
eggshell.

Platform Nest

The Stork

The stork likes to build its nest high
up on platforms, including trees,
buildings or other man-made structures.
Stork nests can be reused year after year
and can reach an impressive size,
measuring up to two meters in
diameter and three meters in depth.
Stork eggs are white.

The Cuckoo

The common cuckoo doesn't build a
nest of its own but places its eggs in other
birds' nests.

The colour and pattern of the cuckoo egg
mimics those of its hosts in order to trick
them into accepting it as their own.

When the cuckoo chick hatches, it grows
very fast and pushes the other eggs or
chicks out of the nest.

The Emperor Penguin

Emperor penguins have to endure one of the world's
worst breeding conditions—the cold Antarctic winter.
Females lay one single egg before they start their
long journey to the sea to feed, only to return once
the chick has hatched.
The male penguins incubate their eggs in large colonies.
Because an egg cannot withstand the freezing cold
of the icy ground, the penguins balance their egg on
their feet and cover it with a warm brood pouch.
Penguins' eggs are a pale greenish white with a
very thick shell.

Insect Eggs

Animals that lay eggs, inside of which the young then
develop before hatching, are called Oviparous.
Birds, reptiles, amphibians, fish, invertebrates and
even some mammals all lay eggs.
Insect eggs are of a very different size and construction
than bird eggs, and the insect parents often just leave
them to survive on their own. As most insect eggs
are not incubated like bird eggs are, they hatch as a result
of environmental temperatures. A warmer temperature
means that the eggs will hatch more quickly.
Many insects lay their eggs in clusters on wood, leaves
or other surfaces, but some insects spread them out
one by one. Insects try to lay their eggs in or on the
food source that the young will eat after they hatch.
Insects can lay hundreds of eggs at the same time.

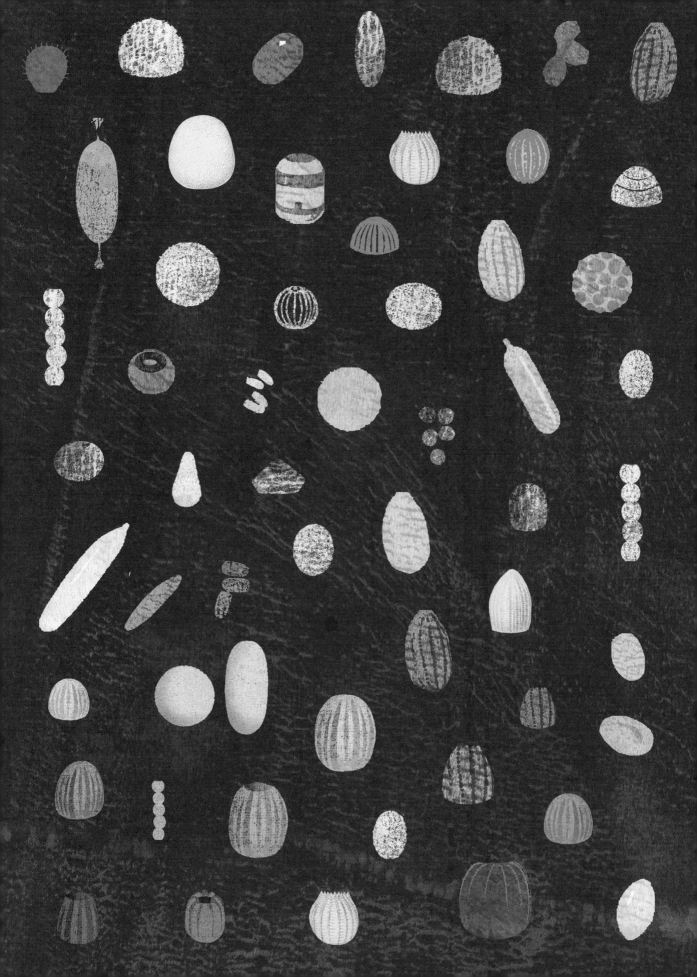

Shapes

Insect eggs can look quite alien
to the human eye.
They come in a dazzling and varied
array of colours and shapes.
They can be globular, smooth,
rough, ridged, spiky, transparent,
opaque, cylindrical, spherical,
oval or cone-shaped.

Frog Spawn

Amphibians

Amphibious frogs lay their eggs in water
so they don't dry up.
Frog spawn is made up of thousands of
single eggs, each one having a tiny black
tadpole embryo surrounded in jelly. Like
insects, frogs generally don't look after
their young. They lay so many eggs
to ensure that some of the embryos will
survive to adulthood.

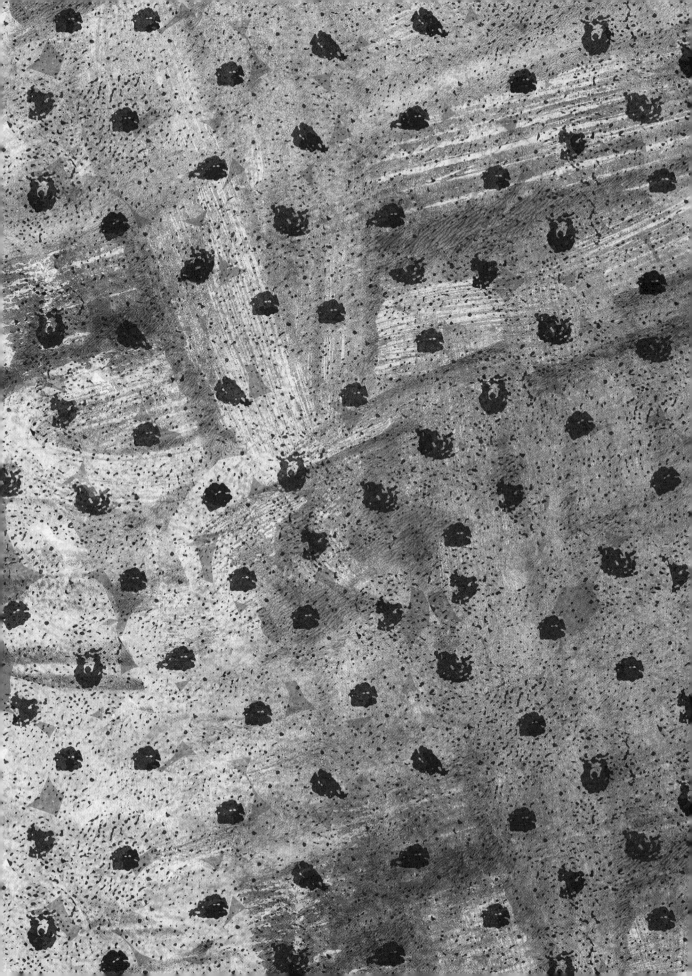

Reptiles

Most reptiles lay soft-shelled eggs, which are incubated by natural heat and do not have to bear the weight of an incubating adult. Reptile eggs are usually hidden and have no need for colour, and most have a creamy white tone. Reptile eggs tend to be symmetrical and do not possess the blunt and pointed end seen in most bird eggs.

Some reptiles guard their nest while others leave their eggs to hatch and develop on their own. Baby reptiles tend to look like a smaller version of their parents when they hatch.

Sea Turtles

Sea turtles have roamed the earth's oceans since the time of the dinosaurs.

There are seven existing species of sea turtles today.

Turtles spend most of their life in the ocean and can migrate thousands of miles between their feeding ground and the beaches where they nest.

During nesting season the adult female will return back to the same beach where she was born. She will dig out a nest in the sand and lay between 50-200 eggs (depending on the species) before returning to the ocean, leaving her eggs to develop on their own in the nest.

It takes between 45 to 70 days for the eggs to hatch and up to a week for a young to dig its way out of the sand.

Hatchlings usually wait until night to emerge from the nest to avoid daytime predators and may use the moonlight and the lighter horizon to find their way to the sea.

Young sea turtles are very vulnerable to predators and only a few survive to adulthood.

Research indicates that the gender of a turtle is determined by the temperature within the nest.

Fish

Trout Eggs

The eggs of a trout can be coloured in
various hues of red, yellow and orange.
Trout lay their eggs in nests (also called redds),
which are built like a little trench in the
gravel of a freshwater lake or stream.
The female builds the redd, usually between
November and January when the water is
cold and carrying lots of oxygen. Trout eggs
need this extra oxygen to hatch.

The Platypus

Platypuses belong to a sub-group of mammals that lay eggs rather than giving birth to live young. They are called monotremes. There are only two mammals on earth that lay eggs—one is the platypus and the other the echidna (which

has four separate species, to be precise). The habitat of both monotremes
is Australia and New Guinea. Scientists believe that these fascinating animals
are the earliest relatives of modern mammals. Recent studies suggest that
they first evolved more than 112 million years ago, well before the extinction
of the dinosaurs.

The Egg in Art, Religion & Mythology

Life wouldn't exist without the egg.

All life springs from it and it's no wonder that the egg
is worshipped around the world as source of all life.
The egg can symbolize birth, new life, fertility and
health, and it also represents rebirth and immortality.
It is surrounded by magical and supernatural beliefs.
In many creation myths from all over the world, the
universe begins as a 'cosmic' egg that is sometimes
fertilized by a serpent. In some stories the upper half
of this egg becomes the sky and the lower half
the earth.

Art and Religion

For Christians, the Easter egg is a symbol of the
resurrection / rebirth of Jesus Christ.
(In Orthodox tradition Easter eggs were died red
to represent his death).
It was custom to place eggs in Christian graves.
In the famous altarpiece by Italian painter Piero della
Francesca ('Madonna and Child with Saints' – c. 1450),
what is believed to be an ostrich egg is hanging over
the Virgin Mary. Scholars still argue over the meaning
of the egg, but it is widely believed to be a symbol
of virginity and resurrection.
Other artists, including Salvador Dalí, Max Ernst,
René Magritte, Constantin Brancusi, Barbara
Hepworth and Leonardo da Vinci, paid homage
to the egg as a source of life.

Mythology

In many myths and legends from all over
the world, gods and heroes have hatched from
an egg.

Maybe the most famous story is that of Leda
and the Swan from Greek mythology. In
this story, the Greek god Zeus turned himself
into a swan and seduced Leda, queen of Sparta.
Leda laid two eggs from which two sets of
twins were born — Polydeuces (Pollux) and
Helen of Troy and Castor and Clytemnestra.

Traditions

There are many egg-related customs all over the world.
Many are based on traditional spring rites that have been
adapted by religion.
The exchange of eggs in the springtime has been practised
for centuries, well before Easter was established.
But most of these traditions are nowadays linked to the
Easter celebrations.
There are Easter egg hunts, egg dancing and Easter egg
rolling. (In Christianity, Easter egg rolling is supposed
to represent the rolling away of the stone from Christ's tomb.)
In some countries, trees, bushes and fountains are decorated
with white or colourfully decorated eggs.
On the UK's Pancake Day, or Shrove Tuesday, people
traditionally used up all of their eggs. This practice took
place because Shrove Tuesday was last day before lent,
a time when Christians were not supposed to eat eggs.

The Fabergé Egg

The world's most expensive Easter eggs are the
Fabergé eggs.

These were pieces of beautiful decorative art created
by Russian jeweller Peter Carl Fabergé.

The costliest Fabergé eggs were those commissioned
by Russian Tsar Alexander III to give to his wife,
the Empress Marie Fedorovna, as a special gift for
Easter. They were called the Imperial Eggs and
were created between 1885 and 1916.

Each of these eggs contains a surprise inside,
like a pure gold hen, a mechanical swan or a golden
miniature of the palace.

Only 50 eggs were made, of which 43 still exist.

The last Imperial Egg on the market was sold for
around 20 million pounds (or 33 million dollars).

Egg Decorating

Egg decoration is an old form of art that has been
around for centuries.

Many cultures around the world have a long and rich
history of decorating eggs to celebrate spring, fertility
and the resurrection of Christ.

Emu and ostrich eggs thought to be thousands of years
old have been found decorated with carvings and engravings.
One of the oldest known globes depicting the world
may be that of an engraved ostrich egg dating back to
the early 1500s.

Whilst ostrich and emu eggs are the preferred eggs
used for carving and engraving due to their thick shell,
many artists today produce delicate lace carvings on
chicken eggs by using tiny drills.

There are many different ways of egg decorating.
Eastern Europeans, for example, adorn chicken, duck
and goose eggs with dyes, wax, scraping and other
forms of decoration to make beautiful works of art.

The Golden Egg

In most countries around the world the egg is a symbol of luck, wealth and health.

The golden egg is a reoccurring theme in many stories and fairy tales all over the globe, including 'Jack and the Beanstalk', Aesop's fable 'The Goose That Laid the Golden Egg', the Russian fairy tale 'The Golden Egg' and the fairy tales collected by German writers Ludwig Bechstein and the Brothers Grimm. There are also countless stories of magical golden eggs guarded by dragons.

© 2017, Prestel Verlag, Munich · London · New York
A member of Verlagsgruppe Random House GmbH
Neumarkter Strasse 28 · 81673 Munich

Prestel Publishing Ltd.
14-17 Wells Street
London W1T 3PD

Prestel Publishing
900 Broadway, Suite 603
New York, NY 10003

Library of Congress Control Number: 2016960246
A CIP catalogue record for this book is available
from the British Library.

Editorial direction: Doris Kutschbach
Copyediting: Brad Finger
Production management: Corinna Pickart
Typesetting: Meike Sellier
Separations: ReproLine Mediateam, Munich
Printing and binding: DZS Grafik, d.o.o., Ljubljana
Paper: Tauro

Verlagsgruppe Random House FSC® N001967

Printed in Slovenia

ISBN 978-3-7913-7294-5
www.prestel.com